1001
Things to Spot
in the Sea

Katie Daynes

Illustrated by Teri Gower

Designed by Natacha Goransky

Edited by Anna Milbourne

Natural history consultant: Dr. Margaret Rostron

Contents

Things to spot

The scenes in this book show seas and oceans from around the world. In each scene there are lots of things for you to find and count.

There is also a puzzle on pages 30 to 31 with even more things to spot in the sea. There are 1001 things for you to spot altogether.

Each little picture shows you what to look for in the big picture.

The blue number tells you how many of that thing you need to find.

Underwater forest

10 garibaldi fish

8 turban snails

5 black rock fish

9 kelp crabs

8 kelp bass

4 sea otters

10 sea urchins

6 sea fans

2 leopard sharks

9 kelp fish

This is Billy. He has explored seas and oceans all over the world. He always takes his underwater camera with him. As you go through the book, see if you can spot Billy's camera in each scene.

Open sea

8 squid   10 mackerel

1 humpback whale

10 sea nettles

8 halfmoon fish

3 ocean sun fish

4 blue sharks

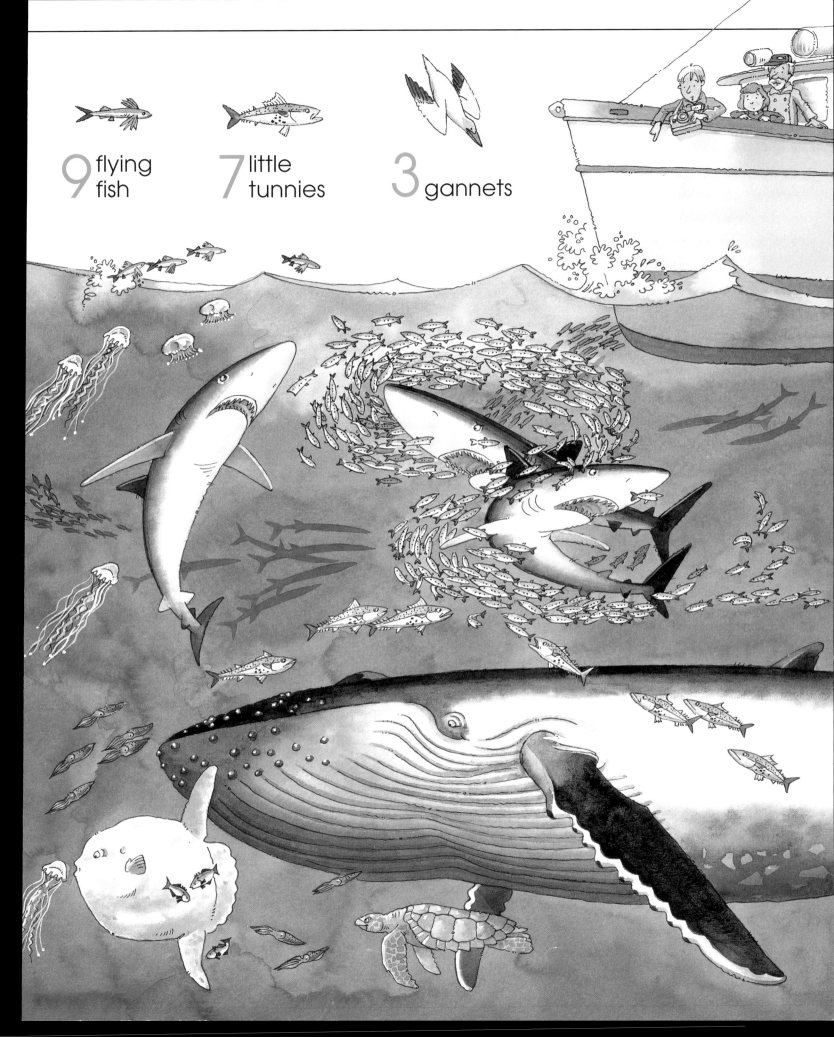

9 flying fish

7 little tunnies

3 gannets

Water sports

4 speedboats 10 flippers 5 jet skis 9 yellow life jackets 3 rubber rings

9 red buoys

6 striped sails

10 herring gulls

5 windsurfers

7 boogy boards

9 snappers 5 roseate spoonbills 8 blue crabs 7 terrapins 10 butterfly fish

Shipwreck

2 writing slates

9 banner fish

10 barracudas

5 carnation corals

9 squirrel fish

10 surgeon fish

7 sweetlips

4 moray eels

1 anchor

8 cow fish

At the aquarium

7 moon jellyfish

Aquariums help you find out about sea animals. This aquarium shows animals from this book. Can you find which scenes they are from and count them all?

10 emperor fish

7 bottlenose dolphins

10 walruses

3 tripod fish

10 red sea anemones

8 macaroni penguins

3 loggerhead turtles

2 napoleon wrasses

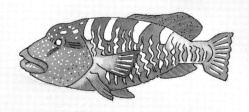

1 blue-spotted ray

8 seahorses

9 picasso fish

6 lion fish

6 spiny lobsters

7 butterfly blennies

5 sun stars

Answers

Did you find all the aquarium animals in the book? Here's where they are.

Posters of animals

7 moon jellyfish:
Open sea
(pages 4 and 5)

10 emperor fish:
Sea village
(pages 20 and 21)

7 bottlenose dolphins:
On a cruise
(pages 16 and 17)

10 walruses:
Icy north
(pages 8 and 9)

3 tripod fish:
Deep down
(pages 18 and 19)

10 red sea anemones:
By the seashore
(pages 12 and 13)

8 macaroni penguins:
Chilly south
(pages 24 and 25)

Animals in tanks

1 blue-spotted ray:
Shipwreck
(pages 28 and 29)

3 loggerhead turtles:
Open sea
(pages 4 and 5)

2 napoleon wrasses:
Shipwreck
(pages 28 and 29)

8 seahorses:
Grassy seabed
(pages 26 and 27)

9 picasso fish:
Coral reef
(pages 10 and 11)

6 lion fish:
Coral reef
(pages 10 and 11)

6 spiny lobsters:
Grassy seabed
(pages 26 and 27)

7 butterfly blennies:
Lost city
(pages 22 and 23)

5 sun stars:
Underwater forest
(pages 14 and 15)

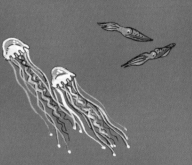

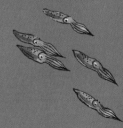

Managing editor: Gillian Doherty
Managing designers: Mary Cartwright and Russell Punter

The publishers would like to thank the following people for their advice:
- Emad Khalil, underwater archaeologist at Southampton University
- Jonathan Mendez, chief powerboat instructor for the Royal Yachting Association
- Rachael Saul from Hebridean Island Cruises Ltd
- Matt Slater, marine biologist at Blue Reef Aquarium, Newquay
- Sally Thomas from The Royal Institute of Naval Architects